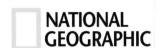
NATIONAL
GEOGRAPHIC

T0045217

Look at the Leaves

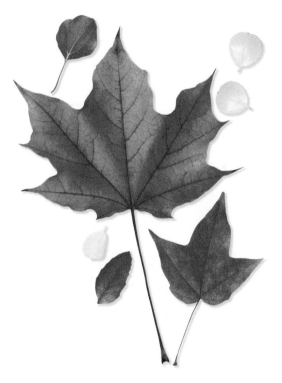

Rachel Griffiths

You can sort the leaves by color.

2

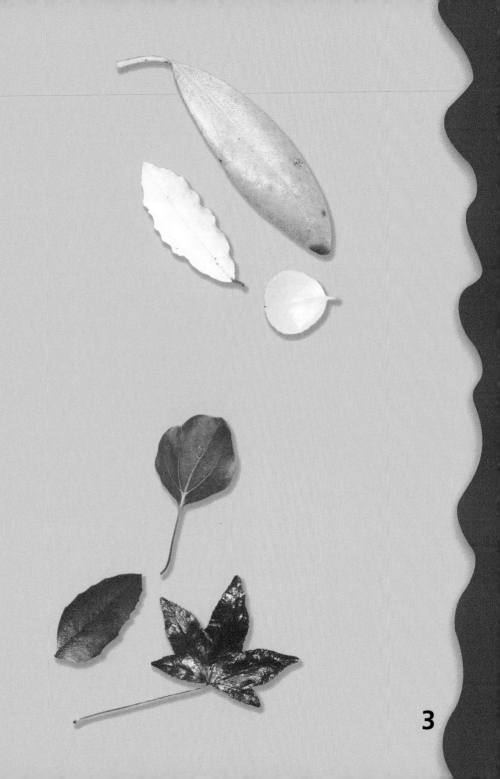

You can sort the leaves by size.

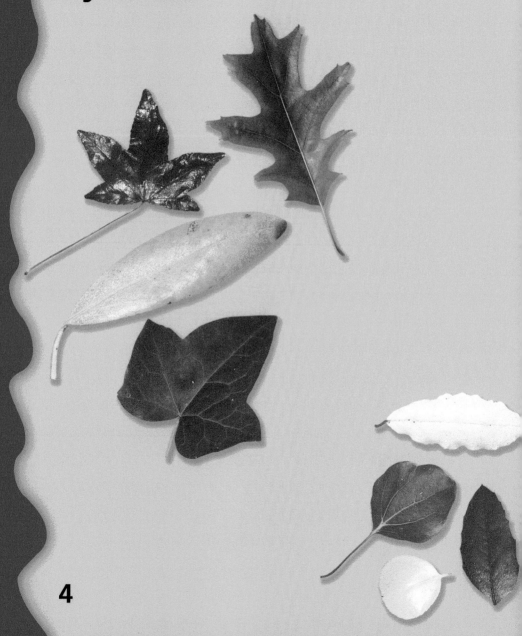

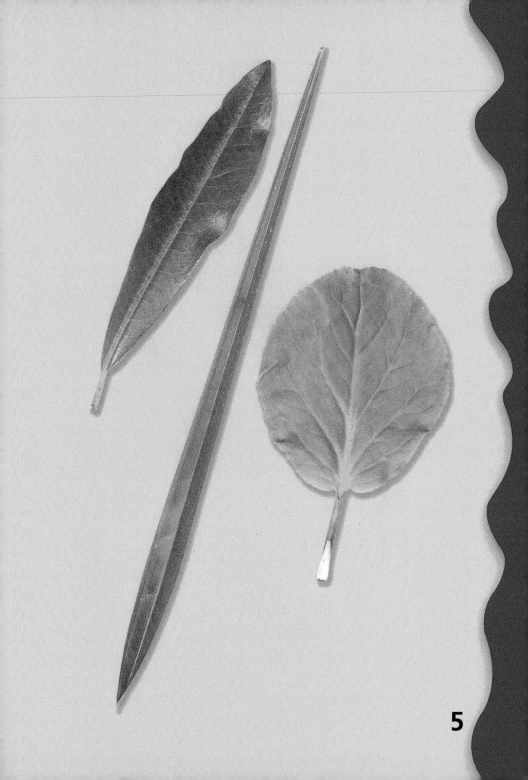

5

You can sort the leaves by **shape**.

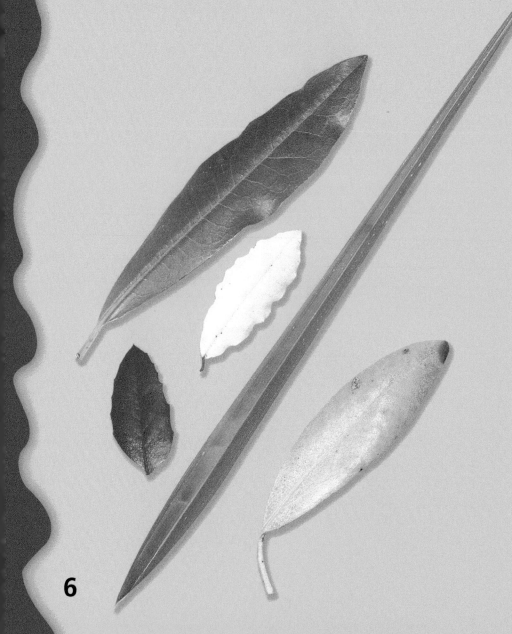

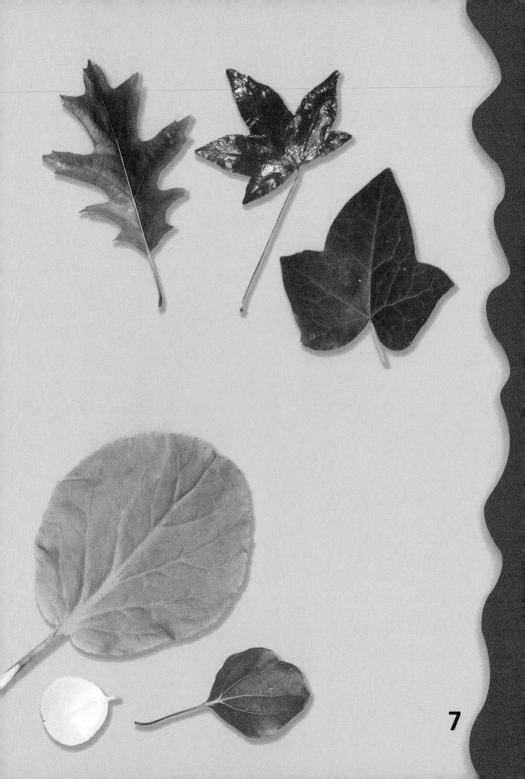

How would you sort the leaves?

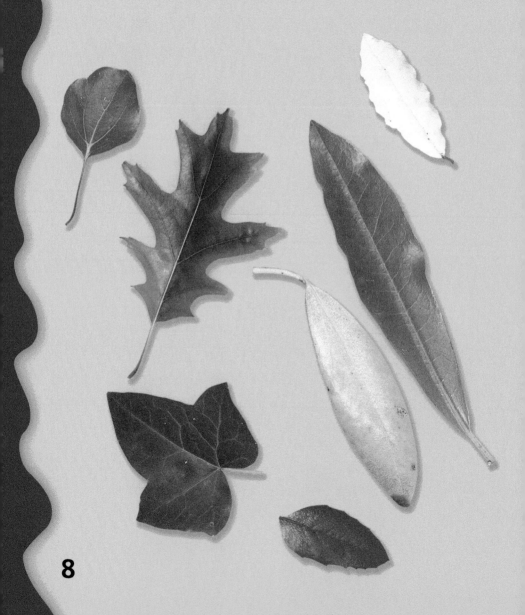